Crazy Canadian Trivia 4

Scholastic Canada Ltd.
604 King Street West, Toronto, Ontario M5V 1E1, Canada

Scholastic Inc.
557 Broadway, New York, NY 10012, USA

Scholastic Australia Pty Limited
PO Box 579, Gosford, NSW 2250, Australia

Scholastic New Zealand Limited
Private Bag 94407, Greenmount, Auckland, New Zealand

Scholastic Children's Books
Euston House, 24 Eversholt Street, London NW1 1DB, UK

Library and Archives Canada Cataloguing in Publication
Hancock, Pat
Crazy Canadian trivia 4 / Pat Hancock ; illustrations by Bill Dickson.

ISBN 978-0-545-98994-9

1. Canada--Miscellanea--Juvenile literature.
I. Dickson, Bill II. Title. III. Title: Crazy Canadian trivia four.
FC58.H285 2009   j971   C2008-906819-X

ISBN-10 0-545-98994-9

6 5 4 3 2 1   Printed in Canada   09 10 11 12 13

Pat Hancock

Crazy Canadian Trivia 4

Illustrations by Bill Dickson

Scholastic Canada Ltd.

Toronto New York London Auckland Sydney
Mexico City New Delhi Hong Kong Buenos Aires

To Chris, John and Mireille, who bring joy
to those I love...

Introduction

After more than thirty years of it, I still love collecting cool, wild, wonderful and just plain wacky facts about Canada and Canadians. And I still enjoy sharing those facts with readers like you.

In this, the fourth *Crazy Canadian Trivia* book, you'll meet Thomas Haliburton, a Canadian author who created a fictional character named Sam Slick in 1835. Sam was always coming up with catchy comments and wise sayings. Some, like "quick as a wink," became so popular we still use them today. Another one that caught on is, "Facts are stranger than fiction."

As you'll soon find out, Sam was right about that. Some of the facts in this book are very strange indeed. I hope you'll have fun reading about them, and about all the other Canadian trivia I couldn't resist collecting. Enjoy!

Pat Hancock

The smallest...

book in the world was produced in May 2007, by Li Yang and Karen Kavanagh, two physicists doing research at Simon Fraser University in Burnaby, British Columbia.

Titled *Teeny Ted from Turnip Town*, it's a fable written by a Canadian artist named Malcolm Douglas Chaplin. The 30-"page" book, just 0.07 millimetres by 0.10 millimetres, is about 20 times smaller than the head of a pin. It was "written" using a focused beam of fast-moving ions, or charged atoms, which "scrapes" just a few layers of atoms off a surface to create the teeny letters.

Yang and Kavanagh produced 100 copies of the book, and anyone with $20 000 can buy a copy. But you can't read it without a special kind of electron microscope, and one of those can cost hundreds of thousands of dollars. So *Teeny Ted from Turnip Town* isn't about to top the bestseller list any time soon. And there's no point looking for it at the local library, not even with a really powerful magnifying glass.

The world's first...

coloured coin put into circulation was the Canadian quarter featuring a red poppy on one side.

The attractive 25-cent piece honouring Canada's war veterans and the 117 000 Canadians who died serving their country made its debut in October 2004 at the Royal Canadian Mint's facilities in Winnipeg, Manitoba. About 30 million of the coins were distributed about two weeks before Remembrance Day on November 11.

To produce the coins, the Mint came up with a new process that applied red paint to the metal well enough that it was supposed to last for one to three years in circulation. Unfortunately, the colour faded or wore off more quickly than expected. But many Canadians chose to save, not spend, the quarters, keeping them as souvenirs of Remembrance Day and keeping the poppies on them red.

If at First You Don't Succeed

The Mint issued another red poppy quarter in October 2008, this time to commemorate the 90th anniversary of the end of the First World War.

These coins — 11 million of them — were also put into circulation just before Remembrance Day. They had gone through a special heating process to "bake" the red paint on the metal so it wouldn't fade the way it had on the 2004 quarters.

Danger! Spy Coins at Work

When the story broke early in 2007, it sounded like something straight out of a James Bond movie. The U.S Department of Defense had issued a warning that certain Canadian coins were a threat to the security of the United States. Reporters with the Associated Press news service tracked down more information about the strange warning and published their findings in May 2007.

Apparently a few American contractors suspected they were being spied on when they made business trips to Canada late in 2005. Because they were working on classified projects for the United States army, they filed reports about their worries with the U.S Department of Defense. And the reason for their suspicions? Some unusual coins with a micro-thin coating had turned up in their pockets and in a rented car. They couldn't identify the hard, clear coating on the coins, but they figured it must be part of a new miniature device that was sending out secret radio signals that could be used to track their movements.

If the Defense Department officials had had the coins tested, they would have found that they weren't emitting any radio signals. They would have recognized the coins as the red poppy quarters that Canada put into circulation in 2004. And they would have realized that the sinister "mysterious coating" was simply a covering over the red paint to stop it from wearing off.

Even if the 25-cent pieces had been tracking devices, how well would they have worked? What good would they have been if the people being spied on had spent them on a cup of coffee or slipped them into a parking meter, and gone merrily on their way?

Getting Squirrelled

Most golfers do everything they can to avoid the golf course hazards deliberately put in place to test their skills. But, in 2004, players at the Riverside Golf Course in Edmonton, Alberta, couldn't seem to find a way around one hazard that had been testing their patience — not how well they played — for several years.

The 10th and the 18th holes were especially hazardous that year. If golf balls landed on the greens there, they might never be seen again, because lurking in the bushes were some sneaky little squirrels that would zip across the grass, pick them up and make off with them before their owners arrived. Even if golfers arrived in time to catch the bushy-tailed thieves red-handed, there wasn't much point in running after them. They knew how ridiculous a human looked chasing a tiny ball-stealing squirrel, especially since the speedy little devils always got away.

Apparently the squirrels stockpiled most of the balls in birds' nests and forgot about them. The ones they remembered — or hadn't stored yet — they chewed on, gnawing off the hard outer layers of plastic right down to the rubber core. But they didn't eat the plastic; they spit it out and kept on chewing. They must have figured that golf balls helped them practise good dental hygiene.

Like beavers and other rodents, squirrels' teeth keep on growing; otherwise, they'd be worn right down gnawing through tough things like tree branches and nutshells. But if rodents don't chew enough, their teeth grow too long. Gnawing on something hard — like a golf ball — grinds down the teeth to keep them at just the right length.

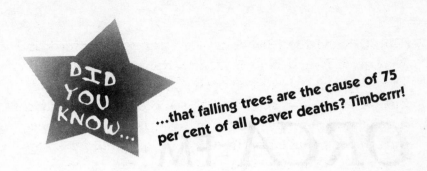

Roadside Rodent

Beaverlodge, Alberta, is a small town about 40 kilometres west of Grand Prairie. In 2004, to celebrate the 75th anniversary of its incorporation, the town decided to put up a welcoming symbol of Beaverlodge at the entrance to the town. And the symbol they chose was — surprise, surprise — a beaver, a really big beaver sitting on a really big log.

At 5.5 metres long, 3 metres wide and 4.6 metres high, the long-toothed, beady-eyed rodent is the biggest beaver in the world.

And it's not surprising to find a 9.8-metre-tall moose named Mac standing beside the highway into Moose Jaw, Saskatchewan, and 8.5-metre-long Ernie the Turtle greeting visitors to Turtleford, Saskatchewan.

ORCA FM

In 1998 the first all-whale radio station in the world started broadcasting killer whales' clicks, moans and whistles from Johnstone Strait on the northeast coast of Vancouver Island.

The signal was strong enough to let people aboard nearby whale-watching boats listen in on the whales' underwater conversations. The sounds were also available to the listening public at 88.5 on the FM dial, thanks to the efforts of John K.B. Ford, a marine scientist studying whale sounds in Johnstone Strait. He had applied for a radio licence in 1997 to broadcast the sounds he was picking up on an underwater microphone as part of his research.

Bye-Bye, Boardwalk – Bonjour, Montreal

In 2008 Hasbro, the toy and game company that makes Monopoly, introduced a new global edition of the game, Monopoly Here and Now: The World Edition. To give the game an international flavour, the company decided that the coloured property spaces would be cities — not streets — from around the world. But they let Monopoly fans decide which cities to choose, inviting them to vote online for their favourite metropolis. Five million ballots were cast, and the cities were ranked according to the number of votes they got. The top 22 became the new properties, and their ranking determined how much they would be worth.

Montreal, Quebec, got the most votes so it's the most expensive property on the World Edition. Vancouver and Toronto also made it to the new board, indicating either that Canadian cities are very popular with Monopoly fans worldwide or that Canadians really like voting online!

The best...

Scrabble player in the world is Canadian Adam Logan.

Born in Kingston, Ontario, in 1975, Logan was already winning Scrabble tournaments when he was just 12 years old. By the time he was 20, he had won both the Canadian and American championships. Ten years later, he claimed the World Championship title, and in 2008 he won his third Canadian National tournament.

Logan was also a mathematical prodigy. When he was 16, he headed to the United States to study math at Princeton University in New Jersey. He graduated summa cum laude, or with highest honours, when he was just 20.

Logan loves mathematics, and he really enjoys playing Scrabble. As he says, "being able to do something very well is fun." Obviously, Logan has lots of fun.

The highest...

streetcar line in the world that crosses
a river runs along the High Level Bridge spanning the
North Saskatchewan River in Edmonton, Alberta.
It's 46 metres high!

A trip aboard one of the old-fashioned streetcars that
rolls along the line isn't just a way for residents to
cross the river — it's also a popular tourist attraction.
The ride in a vintage tram is great fun, and the view is
breathtaking.

But being so high up on such a narrow track with no
barriers or guardrails on either side can be a bit too
breathtaking for some people. It's not unusual for a few
riders to keep their eyes tightly closed for most of
the trip.

High-Wire Act

Anyone nervous about riding across Edmonton's High Level Bridge in a streetcar probably doesn't even want to think about dangling in a gondola, or cable car, nearly half a kilometre above the ground.

But that's the experience awaiting riders aboard the cable cars connecting two mountains that tower above the world-famous ski resort at Whistler, British Columbia. Known as the Whistler Blackcomb Peak 2 Peak Gondola, the cable car system that cost $52 million opened in December 2008.

The actual wire rope that carries the cars is 5.6 centimetres thick and stretches just over three kilometres between two of the tall metal towers, or pylons, that support it, the longest free span in the world. Twenty-eight cars travel across the valley at 7.5 metres a second, and the crossing takes 11 minutes. And if any gondola trip that high and long weren't exciting enough, two of the 28 cars offer riders an extra thrill — the middle sections of their floors are made of glass.

Summertime Suppertime

Lip-Smacking Good

Shediac, New Brunswick, is a town just east of
Moncton on the shore of Northumberland Strait. About
5500 people live in the town, but every year, during the
first week of July, nearly 50 000 visitors show up. They
come to watch parades, listen to great Maritime
musicians, ride the latest midway attractions and swim
in the warmest salt water north of Virginia. But most of
all, they come to feast on the hard-shelled, big-clawed,
beady-eyed, antenna-waving seafood treasure for which
Shediac is famous. They come to eat lobster — served
up at lobster suppers held each evening of the Lobster
Festival.

Each night three visitors are chosen to enter a lobster-
eating contest. The winner is the fastest one to crack
open, pull apart and eat three lobsters — using bare
hands alone. The cheering crowds love watching the
messy race to reach the tasty flesh inside, and the
three volunteers are more than willing to entertain
them — because in this contest even the losers win.
They get to eat three lobsters for free.

And while they're in the Lobster Capital of the World, most visitors also check out the huge concrete sculpture in the park at the west end of town — a 5-metre-wide and nearly 11-metre-long 50-tonne lobster poised to give a 1.8-metre-tall fisherman a mighty big claw hug. The huge crustacean is the biggest lobster in the world. Nearly half a million people stop to look at it each year. And quite a few of them also drop by Shediac's other big sculpture — a huge white rooster in front of a fried chicken restaurant.

Save Big Dee-Dee

Another big lobster drew crowds to Shediac, New Brunswick, early in July 2008, when Denis Breau, owner of The Big Fish seafood shop and market, announced that he was going to auction off a very rare catch — a 100-year-old monster lobster weighing 10 kilograms. Breau set the starting bid at $1000, figuring some large restaurant might want to pay big bucks for it as a publicity stunt. The lobster's size and the high starting bid made the news, and within two weeks more than 1000 visitors had dropped by The Big Fish to see the big catch, which had been nicknamed Big Dee-Dee.

But as news spread that Big Dee-Dee was probably destined for a big pot of boiling water, an Internet campaign to save the huge lobster began, attracting the kind of publicity Denis Breau could have done without. The last thing he had wanted was to be seen as a greedy animal-hater, ready to end the life of a senior citizen of the sea, but some harassing phone callers were treating him as if that's exactly what he was.

Laura-Leah Shaw, a real estate agent from Vancouver, British Columbia, offered to buy Big Dee-Dee for $1000, along with two other anonymous bidders from Ontario who were ready to kick in $2000, just so the captive crustacean could swim free. As more offers came in, reporters from as far away as Europe started taking an interest in Big Dee-Dee's fate. But Breau decided he'd had enough of being caught in the media spotlight. He changed his mind about selling the mega lobster to the highest bidder, and arranged for him to live out the rest of his days in the comfort of an aquarium at the Huntsman Marine Science Centre in St. Andrews, New Brunswick. Here Big Dee-Dee could still be a big tourist attraction, but Breau wouldn't be, and that was fine with him.

We Can't Believe It Finally Looks Like Butter

In the summer of 2008, after 21 years of being the only province in Canada where making or selling yellow-tinted margarine was still illegal, the Quebec government finally lifted the ban against *la margarine jaune*. Before then, if Quebecers preferred spreading a sunny-coloured version of the popular non-dairy product on their muffins, they had to sneak it into the province.

Until the 1960s, yellow-coloured margarine had been banned in many places around the world, mainly because

Margarine or Butter?

dairy farmers argued that its introduction would seriously cut into sales of butter. It was easier to spread and a lot less expensive. The ban was also an attempt to stop crooks from selling "fake" butter — high-priced margarine made and packaged to taste and look like butter, and priced like it too. But by 2008 the Quebec government figured people could tell the difference and were entitled to make their own choice about the colour of the spread melting on their warm toast.

A Slam Dunk

The high school basketball game played in Toronto on February 7, 2002, between teams from West Hill Collegiate and R.H. King Academy was a blowout. West Hill won 150-58, thanks to the amazing play of a 1.96-metre-tall player named Denham Brown. Brown was hot that night. He sank 13 three-pointers! By the end of the first quarter he had scored 40 points. He scored another 41 in the third quarter, and by the end of the game, had chalked up a grand total of 111 points — the highest number of points ever scored by a Canadian basketball player.

Grab a Shovel

According to Environment Canada, more snow falls in Toronto on Thursdays than on other days of the week, and a one-day snowfall of more than 10 centimetres in the city is unusual.

But in January 1999 something unusual happened. Starting with a 39-centimetre snowfall on January 2 and a 26-centimetre one on January 14, by the end of the month the city had received 118.4 centimetres, the heaviest one-month snowfall ever recorded for Toronto.

In fact so much snow fell that the city was having trouble keeping downtown streets clear and finding places to put the plowed snow. When emergency vehicles couldn't navigate the clogged streets, Mayor Mel Lastman called in the armed forces to help city workers with the cleanup. Nearly 450 troops and close to 130 military vehicles arrived from Petawawa, Ontario, and Prince Edward Island lent the city 15 big snow blowers. It took nearly two weeks for Toronto to dig itself out, and snow-clearing costs for the month totalled a whopping $70 million.

Planning Ahead

Some people living in Montreal and Ottawa made fun of Toronto for calling in the army to help them cope with the snow in January 1999. These cities are used to dealing with heavier snowfalls and proud of the very efficient snow-clearing plans they have in place.

Churchill Falls, Labrador, one of the top 10 snowiest places in Canada, has one of the coolest plans for dealing with snow removal. In the late 1960s, when permanent homes were built for employees of the massive new hydroelectric power station here, they were located on only one side of each street. That leaves plenty of space on the opposite side to push the metres of plowed snow that build up over the winter.

The deepest amount of snow ever measured at a weather station in Canada was at Grouse Mountain, British Columbia. The snow was 9.68 metres deep there on April 8, 1999.

St. John's, Newfoundland, was buried under the biggest one-day snowfall in a major Canadian city when 68.4 centimetres buried the province's capital on April 5, 1999.

And on December 29, 1996, 64.5 centimetres fell on Victoria, the capital of British Columbia.

Only one major Canadian city has had a snowfall in every single month of the year, even in June, July and August. That distinction belongs to Calgary, Alberta.

GHOULISH SCHOOL SUPPLIES

Back in the 1870s, several students attending medical school at McGill University in Montreal, Quebec, were often short of funds to pay their tuition fees. As well, back then, the medical school was often short of the corpses that students dissected to learn everything they could about human anatomy. So, to make extra money, some students would slip into the cemetery on the west side of Mount Royal late at night, dig up the bodies of poor people who had died recently, and sell them to the college for up to $50 each — a lot of money back then.

But before the students took the bodies away, they removed the clothes they'd been buried in. Anyone caught stealing bodies simply had to pay a fine because corpses weren't considered property. But stealing property such as clothes and shoes was criminal, and the body snatchers didn't want to be charged with and convicted of theft.

Ghostly Blame

Some people believe that the cemeteries on Montreal's Mount Royal are haunted. Apparently ghosts have been seen drifting around the boundaries of the burial grounds, and over the years there have been reported sightings of a ghost flying down the mountainside on a toboggan. The following paragraph might explain why such a spooky story came to be associated with that location. It's part of a description that a highly respected physician and anatomy professor, Dr. Francis J. Shepherd, wrote about how bodies arrived in his dissecting lab during the winter months in the 1870:

"The students went up at night, disinterred the bodies buried usually the previous morning, removed all clothing, wrapped them in blankets and tobogganed them down Côte des Neiges Hill. Many weird tales are told of accidents and the bodies rolling off the toboggan, and people who saw the accident thinking a death had occurred."

No wonder weird tales were told and rumours about toboggan-riding ghosts began to spread.

But on a more serious note, people may have found it easier to blame supernatural activity than to accept that Montreal and other Canadian cities didn't have a proper, respectful system for making corpses available to medical schools. Such a system was put in place in Canada in 1883, and by the next year grave-robbing for medical studies had come to an end.

Seating 10 000 People — 6 at a Time

Those words are on a sign outside the church in Drumheller, Alberta, known simply as The Little Church. At just 2.1 metres long and 3.4 metres wide, it may very well be the smallest church in the world. It is a tourist attraction, but it's also a place of worship, and anyone hoping to have a really, really small wedding might want to check it out. It has just six one-person pews, and there's barely enough room for the happy couple and the minister to stand at the front.

One-of-a-Kind Dinosaur Find

Drumheller, Alberta, has another tourist attraction that draws much bigger crowds than The Little Church does. Located about 140 kilometres northeast of Calgary, the town gets nearly half a million visitors each year because it's home to the world-famous Royal Tyrrell Museum of Paleontology. The museum displays one of the world's finest collections of dinosaur fossils. The town is also home to the world's largest dinosaur — a model that people can climb inside. Nine storeys tall, the T-rex towers above the surrounding badlands.

Several much smaller sculptures of other dinosaurs, such as Triceratops and Stegosaurus, are located in the town itself, providing tourists with some great photo ops. Two of those sculptures are particularly interesting. They depict Smileasaurus Banana Eater and Shysasaurus Jelly Bean Eater, dinosaurs so rare that no one outside Drumheller had ever heard of them before their statues were revealed. Their skeletons were discovered deep in the imagination of an artist with a good sense of humour.

Big Art on Display

Trygve "Tig" Seland, a contractor and artist who lived in Drumheller, created many of the dinosaur sculptures placed around his hometown. He also designed and erected The Little Church.

But Drumheller isn't the only place in Alberta where you can see examples of Seland's artistic efforts. He designed Aaron, the 2.4-metre-high great blue heron that welcomes visitors to Barrhead, a small town in northern Alberta. He also designed three large sculptures of magnificent grey geese taking off, flying and landing in Hanna, and Eddie, a 2.4-metre-tall red squirrel in Edson.

East Coast Boast

People live longer in Nova Scotia than in other parts of Canada. More people get to celebrate their 100th birthday here, especially in Lunenburg and Yarmouth, than in any other place in the country. On average, 14 to 15 per 100 000 Canadians reach that major milestone, but as many as 50 per 100 000 living in these two Nova Scotia towns get to be centenarians.

The happiest Canadians also live in the Maritimes. Research completed in 2007 revealed that Saint John, New Brunswick, was the most livable city in Canada and the happiest Canadians were living there. Quebec City was number two on the happy people/livable cities list, but three other east coast cities — Charlottetown in Prince Edward Island, Moncton in New Brunswick and St. John's in Newfoundland — were ranked third, fourth and fifth.

So if you're looking for a place where you can be happy and grow very old, maybe you should say hello, not farewell, to Nova Scotia or one of the other three Atlantic provinces.

Blue Gold

Maybe people in Nova Scotia eat lots of blueberries. They're supposed to be good for your eyes, your heart, your brain, your colon and various other body parts that start to fail as you grow older, and this province grows a lot of them.

Nova Scotia, along with British Columbia and Quebec, is a world leader in wild blueberry production, and some research shows that wild blueberries are even better for you than cultivated ones.

More and more, people around the world are turning to both kinds of berries as healthy snacks, and blueberry production is booming. By 2007 nearly 227 million kilograms were being produced worldwide. That's a lot of blueberries! By 2008 the small blue berries had become the most valuable fruit crop in Canada.

DID YOU KNOW...

...that Canadian hockey superstar Wayne Gretzky loved playing baseball more than hockey when he was young? He did very well playing shortstop and pitching for local kids' teams in Brantford, and when he was just 10, was quoted as saying, "If I couldn't play hockey, I'd like to play baseball with the Oakland Athletics and [their star pitcher] Vida Blue." But Gretzky could play hockey — wow, could he play hockey — so he did, and baseball's loss was hockey's gain.

IT'S A BIRD?
IT'S A PLANE?
IT'S A MYSTERY

Whatever people observed in the early evening skies above the north coast of Prince Edward Island on December 26, 2007, they were absolutely certain of one thing — they had never seen anything like it before. Two witnesses, Tony and Marie (Ford) Quigley of North Tryon, P.E.I., were driving home when they spotted it, and hurried into the house to get their video camera.

What they watched, and caught on tape, was a small shiny orb moving down slowly — not plunging — from high in the sky, with what looked like dark smoke trailing behind. After a few minutes the object appeared to lengthen and to spiral or twist downward, leaving huge clouds of smoke in its wake. After nearly half an hour, the strange object disappeared from view.

For the next several weeks, the Quigleys tried to find out what they and a few others had watched that night. They showed their tape to reporters, and contacted the local RCMP detachment and officials at the airport in Charlottetown and at Environment Canada. But no one could explain what they had seen. No meteor or comet had flashed across the Maritime skies around dinnertime on December 26, 2007. No secretly launched rocket had exploded, and no piece of space junk had burned up as it fell to Earth.

Eventually the Quigleys accepted the fact that they would probably never know exactly what they had observed. They had joined the ranks of those who report seeing a UFO — an unidentified flying object high in the night sky.

...that, according to the UFOlogy Research Centre in Winnipeg, Manitoba, fewer people are reporting seeing flying saucers? Most reported UFOs are still described as being small, round and shiny, but sightings of flying triangles are on the rise.

Research also shows that more UFO sightings are reported in the summer than in the winter. Surprise, surprise. When would most people prefer to stand outside staring at the night sky? Not when the temperature dips below zero, that's for sure.

TV's Reality Comes to Town

The Ruby Café was just to the left of the gas station at the corner of Highway 39 and Grid Road #714. You could stroll past the Dog River Hotel, the offices of The Howler newspaper, and the FOO   MAR   T grocery store with a D, K and E missing from its sign. If you were looking for a police officer, there was no point going into the police station on Main Street. A tourist might have made that mistake, but local residents wouldn't have. They knew that the building behind the Dog River Municipal Police sign was actually a café called The Stoop, and that the closest real police station was 40 kilometres away from their hometown of Rouleau (not Dog River), Saskatchewan.

For nearly seven years, from 2002 to 2008, Rouleau led a double life. In the real world it was a small town of about 400 people in Saskatchewan, 100 kilometres northwest of Weyburn. In the fictional world of TV sitcoms it was Dog River, a small Saskatchewan town in the middle of nowhere. The words "Dog River" were even painted on the grain elevator, leaving some real-life tourists scratching their heads when they ended up in Rouleau but couldn't find Dog River on a map.

But the award-winning TV comedy *Corner Gas*, which is set in Dog River, put Rouleau on the map in a big way. Sets depicting the gas station and the Ruby Café were erected, signs saying Dog River were put up on several of the town's buildings, and film crews shot the show's outdoor scenes all around the town. Crowds of tourists showed up each spring and summer, snapping pictures of themselves in front of Dog River's familiar landmarks and hoping for a chance to see the show's stars at work. It's estimated that more than $700 000 flowed into Rouleau because of the show's presence here during its highly successful six-season run.

In 2008 comedian Brent Butt, the creator and co-star of *Corner Gas*, decided he wanted the show to end while it was still enormously popular, and that September the cast and crew finished filming the final season's last episodes. But by then episodes of *Corner Gas* airing in 27 countries were receiving rave reviews, ensuring that the show's presence would continue to be felt in Rouleau.

As long as the town leaves Dog River painted on its grain elevator, tourists from far and wide will still manage to make their way to the little town in the middle of nowhere that isn't marked on any map.

...that Brent Butt set his hit show in his home province?

Butt was born and raised in Tisdale, a small town a four-hour drive north of Regina. The two actors who played his character's parents on the show are Saskatchewanians too. Eric Peterson, who played his grumpy dad, Oscar, was born in Indian Head, Saskatchewan, and Janet Wright, Brett's TV mom, Emma, grew up in Saskatoon.

...that *Little Mosque on the Prairie,* another hugely popular Canadian TV sitcom, also takes place in a little town in Saskatchewan, in this case a fictional place called Mercy? Like *Corner Gas, Little Mosque* has become a hit with viewers in more than two dozen countries around the world.

Chilly Dip

On January 19, 2004, Wang Gangyi, a 48-year-old law professor from China, showed up at Bay Bulls, Newfoundland, with a film crew in tow. Wang had come to Newfoundland to honour the memory of the people who died when the *Titanic* sank off the coast of Newfoundland on April 14, 1912. To do so, he threw some memorial wreaths into the icy Atlantic, and then he jumped in after them.

But Wang didn't take a quick in-and-out plunge the way Polar Bear Club folks do each New Year's Day. Oh no. He swam around in the 0.7ºC waters for 37 minutes and 30 seconds, another record for China's most famous ice swimmer.

The deadliest ...

heat wave in Canada took place in 1936, in the midst of a terrible drought. It gripped the country from July 5 to July 17, claiming the lives of 1180 Canadians.

There's a First Time for Everything

On August 16, 2008, hundreds of people gathered in Whistler, British Columbia, for the first annual Canadian Cheese Rolling Festival.

Inspired by the famous Cooper's Hill Cheese Rolling races held each May near Gloucester, England, organizers set the course on a long, wide slope with room enough along the sides for spectators to watch the crazy, funny and potentially dangerous event.

On race day many of the participants showed up wearing appropriately cheesy costumes. The smart ones also wore helmets and pads for their knees and elbows. When the racers were lined up at the top of the hill, a special B.C.-made five-kilogram round of cheese was released one second before they took off.

The cheese rolled and bounced down the hill chased by contestants running, stumbling and tumbling after it. But the whole point of the bizarre event wasn't to catch the cheese. The winner was the first person to beat the cheese to the finish line and live to brag about it. And the prize? A five-kilogram wheel of very yummy cheese!

The Little House that Could

In the early hours of July 19, 1996, rain started falling on the Saguenay—Lac-Saint-Jean region of Quebec, north of Quebec City. It poured down all through the night and into the next day, and through to the morning of the 21st. By then as much as 280 millimetres had fallen on the area, producing the worst flood in Canada's history.

Dams burst, dikes failed, and rivers overflowed, spilling torrents of water onto land that was already waterlogged. Sixteen thousand people fled the area as raging rivers gouged out tonnes of mud and rocks, uprooted huge trees, tossed trucks and cars around like bath toys, and washed away entire houses.

But in the midst of the horrific disaster, one little white house in Chicoutimi stood out as a symbol of the people's strength and the region's determination to survive against all odds. Racing water washed away everything around it and surged through its lower floor, but with its foundation built on solid rock, it didn't budge.

Amazing footage of that little house standing firm as torrents of water surrounded it were part of every newscast about the disaster airing around the world. Once the cleanup in Chicoutimi was underway, people started showing up to stare in awe at the place and to photograph it.

Years later, people still come to see it. As a waterfall continues to pour through its front door, it has become a museum dedicated to recording the story of the worst flood in Canadian history.

Another House that Could

The flood waters moving towards the home of Jules and Lucy Mourant in the spring of 1997 weren't torrential. They moved silently and steadily, getting higher by the hour. But with the help of more than three dozen friends and strangers, the Mourants had built a four-metre-high wall of sandbags around their house, hoping it would hold back the rapidly rising water heading their way.

The Mourants lived in St. Norbert, Manitoba, a town located along the Red River about a twenty-minute drive south of Winnipeg. And anyone living along the Red River has to at least think about, if not prepare for, the possibility of coping with the river flooding in the spring when the snow and ice begin to melt. A system of dikes, built-up banks, canals, and a 47-kilometre-long channel around Winnipeg is in place to divert the Red's rising waters, but it can't stop it from overflowing.

The spring runoff was especially heavy in April 1997, and the only thing that could have kept the Mourants' house dry was their sandbag dike. And it did! The house was completely surrounded by water for several days, but the Mourants didn't mind being stuck inside. Their home was safe and they were dry.

Just
the
Stats

During the 1997 Red River flood, 28 000 people were evacuated. About 2000 or so cows and 45 000 laying hens were also moved to safety.

All Dried Up

The Saguenay River Flood in 1996 caused $1 billion in damages, and damage from the 1997 Red River flood topped $800 million. But even though there have been more than 240 disastrous floods in Canada since 1900, many of them catastrophic, six of the ten most expensive natural disasters in the country's history were caused by a *lack* of rain — not by too much of it.

In 1988, for example, a drought on the prairies cost those provinces $1.8 billion, and the 1979-80 drought there cost $2.5 billion. The worst prairie drought on record lasted from 1931 to 1938, a devastatingly dry period that came to be known as the "dirty thirties." About a quarter of a million people were driven from the area by the eight-year dry spell that brought with it parched soil, failed crops, dead livestock, plagues of grasshoppers, grass fires and dust storms.

The largest...

sword fight in the world was staged by students from Ryerson University in Toronto, Ontario, on August 26, 2008.

The crowd of more than 900 eager combatants chanted "We want a sword fight!" while waiting for organizers to finish registering. When they were finally given the green light, they held their blue plastic swords high, cheered, and charged each other. For 12 consecutive minutes, they fought boldly and bravely until they had smashed the current Guinness sword-fighting record and were ordered to lay down their arms.

The most . . .

snow angels in the world made at the same time were counted up in London, Ontario, in February 2004.

The attempt to break the record for the most snow angels attracted a more bundled-up — and mainly younger — crowd than the one that showed up for the sword fight. Parents and teachers, not just kids, were among the 15 851 folks from 60 London District Catholic School Board schools who all dropped to the ground at once and started swooshing their arms and legs in the snow.

This feat was definitely a record breaker! The previous record — 2282 snow angels made simultaneously at eight schools — had been set by a smiling, rosy-cheeked crowd from the Ottawa-Carleton District School Board on March 7, 2003.

Giant Pumpkins Ride the Waves

The giant pumpkins that farmer Howard Dill started growing in the 1980s put his hometown of Windsor, Nova Scotia, on the map. His monstrous gourds broke four world records and growers from around the world ordered seeds that he bred — Atlantic Giants — to grow their own pumpkins weighing more than 600 kilograms. Windsor also became the place for hopeful farmers from across eastern Canada to bring their orange mammoths each October, to see which one weighs the most.

And in 1999 Windsor became the first place in the world
to hold a pumpkin regatta, or boat race. Each year since
then, on the same weekend as the weigh-in, crowds of
visitors come to Windsor to watch dozens of brave souls
struggle to race hollowed-out pumpkins across Pesaquid
Lake.

Not everyone makes it across. The veggie boats are very
difficult to steer, no matter how hard their owners
paddle. They spin and slosh from side to side, and some
just tip over and sink.

But winning isn't everything. Contestants have as much fun as the spectators at this event, which has become so popular that it's not just the world's first pumpkin regatta — it's also the world's largest.

The largest . . .
exporter of mustard seed in the world is Canada.

Canada is the source of 75 to 80 per cent of the world's supply of mustard, and nearly 90 per cent of the mustard seed produced in Canada comes from the province of Saskatchewan. Saskatchewan grows more than 90 per cent of the brown seeds used to make the world-famous Dijon mustard.

Tweet, Tweet

About 80 per cent of the world's supply of canary seed is grown on the Canadian prairies.

Canary seed is a particular type of tall grass that produces seeds covered with a shiny yellow coat, or hull. There's really only one use for canary seed: it's the main ingredient of bird food mixtures. Both caged and wild birds are attracted to its yellow hulls, and they seem to like its taste too.

Kitty Cats Camp Out on Parliament Hill

For as long as anyone can remember, stray cats of all sizes and colours have been hanging out on Parliament Hill in Ottawa. At one time some of them earned their keep chasing after mice inside the Parliament Buildings, but as their numbers increased they became more of a nuisance than the rodents and in 1955 they were evicted.

The cats liked the neighbourhood so they didn't go far. Instead they formed a wild, or feral, cat colony, hunting for their own food and accepting handouts from passersby and outdoor workers. In the 1970s a woman named Irene Desormeaux began bringing them food on a regular basis, and in the 1980s another cat lover named René Chartrand started helping her care for them. But Chartrand didn't just feed the more than two dozen feral felines. He built them little wooden apartments.

In 2008, at 86, Chartrand was still showing up almost every day to feed the 12 or so remaining cats that called his kitty condos home. And as long as there are still cats hanging out on Parliament Hill, volunteers will care for them and tourists will pay them a visit when they check out the Hill.

First-Class Feline Care

A few stray cats that showed up on Parliament Hill have gone to live in far more impressive homes than the wooden structures René Chartrand built.

Every now and then Prime Minister Stephen Harper would take one home to 24 Sussex Drive, the official residence of the leader of Canada's government. There, Mr. Harper and his wife, Laureen, both cat lovers, would give the wild creature extra care and affection until it was comfortable living with humans. Then it could be adopted by someone ready to give it a permanent home.

Mr. Harper also brought home the occasional stray when he and his family lived at Stornoway, the residence of the leader of the official Opposition.

It's Official

Canada was the first country in the British Commonwealth — even before Great Britain itself — to recognize the position of leader of the Opposition.

The Opposition leader was, and still is, usually the leader of the party with the second-most number of votes. But the job was just traditional, not official, until 1905. That year the Canadian government finally passed a law that made leader of the Opposition an official post with a salary and an allowance covering the expenses needed to do the job. Britain — the model for Canada's government — didn't pass a law like that until 1937.

No Thanks!

Even though Stornoway is a very nice house — a fully furnished mansion worth about $2 million — complete with staff to cook, clean and drive for its official residents, one leader of the Opposition refused to live there.

When the Liberals led by Jean Chrétien won the federal election held in October 1993, the party with the next-highest number of seats was the Bloc Québécois. So the Bloc became the official Opposition and its leader, Lucien Bouchard, became Opposition leader.

Bouchard took the additional pay that comes with the job, but he didn't take Stornoway. Since he was leader of the party that wanted Quebec to become independent of, or separate from, Canada, Bouchard refused to move into a residence owned by Canada and paid for by Canadians. Instead, he found a place to live across the Ottawa River in Hull, Quebec.

Jean Chrétien's Liberals won the election held in June 1997 too, and that time the Reform Party led by Preston Manning won enough seats to become the official Opposition.

Before the election Manning had often complained about government wasting taxpayers' money and giving special bonuses, or perks, to many people on Parliament Hill. So, afraid that he'd look like a phony, right after the election Manning said that he didn't want to move into a mansion. He said it was much too fancy for him and his family. But, after a few weeks, he changed his mind and went along with the tradition of the Opposition leader living rent-free in Stornoway, one of the perks that comes with the job.

Royal Refugees

Before Stornoway became the Opposition leader's official home in 1950, it was home to the first member of a royal family ever to be born in North America. Margriet, the royal baby, was born in Ottawa on January 19, 1943. Her royal mum was Dutch Crown Princess Juliana, who was next in line to become queen of the Netherlands.

Juliana's mother, Queen Wilhelmina, had escaped to
England when Nazi Germany invaded the Netherlands in
May 1940, and stayed there until World War II ended.
But to keep her only child — the heir to the throne —
as safe as possible, she sent Juliana and her two
children to live in Ottawa with Canada's Governor
General until she found a house to rent — Stornoway.

A Royal Thank You

During her stay in Canada, Princess Juliana insisted on living like other Canadians, sending her girls to public schools, shopping for her family's groceries and waiting her turn for service. There was one time when she did get special treatment. That was when baby Margriet was born at the Ottawa Civic Hospital. The rooms where the Princess delivered the baby were declared to be extraterritorial, or outside Canada's control and laws; otherwise, the baby would have been born Canadian, not Dutch — the citizenship of her mother — and wouldn't have been in line to succeed her.

The Dutch royal family moved back to the Netherlands after the war ended in 1945. Back home, Princess Juliana arranged to send Canadians a very special thank-you gift for giving her refuge — 100 000 tulip bulbs to be planted in Ottawa, and another 20 000 each year after that. Juliana became queen in 1948. It is thanks to her Royal Highness that nearly one million tulips bloom in Ottawa each May, when the annual Tulip Festival is held.

The best...

country in the world to see the northern lights is Canada.

Because northern Canada is so close to the North Pole and has such low levels of light pollution, it's the best place to view the spectacularly beautiful aurora borealis.

Oink, Oink

Pigs don't drink tea, they don't water gardens, and they certainly don't take baths. In fact, they do very few things that consume water. On average, one Canadian pig uses just 7 to 8 litres of water a day hanging out on a pig farm. That's how much Canadian humans use just washing their hands under a running tap.

On average, a Canadian uses about 340 litres of water a day, at least forty-two times as much as a pig's daily consumption and more than three times as much as a Dane uses in Denmark. *Oink, oink...*

What's Cooking?

There was nothing trivial about the Matheson Fire in July 1916. Also known as the Great Fire of 1916, it was Ontario's deadliest forest fire. It claimed at least 240 lives and left hundreds homeless as it roared through more than 202 000 hectares of northern Ontario. At times the front edge of the blaze was nearly 65 kilometres wide, engulfing everything in its path. Several towns north of Timmins, including Matheson, Cochrane, and Iroquois Falls, were reduced to ashes.

But one small group of survivors who had lost
everything discovered an unexpected side effect of
the fire. As they searched for something to eat, they
came across some chickens in a field that had escaped
the flames. The chickens were dead. They were
roasted too. The heat had also cooked potatoes that
had been growing in the field. So, while waiting several
days for help to arrive, the survivors didn't go hungry.
They ate the chickens first, and then dug up, and into,
the baked potatoes.

Polar Bear

Retirement Home

Cochrane, Ontario, was rebuilt after the Great Fire of
1916. Located about 100 kilometres north of Timmins,
the town of about 5300 serves as the starting point of
an amazing train trip (formerly the Polar Bear Express)
that ends 300 kilometres farther north at Moosonee on
James Bay. Each summer tourists make the trip in
hopes of seeing polar bears in the wild.

But if they miss them in Moosonee, they can still see
some up close at the Cochrane Polar Bear Habitat. They
can even swim with them there! The Habitat, which
opened in 2004, features a large wading pool separated
from the bears' enclosure by a super-thick glass wall.
When the bears swim up to the see-through wall,
waders — especially young ones — on the other side
experience the thrilling sensation of sharing the pool
with the magnificent snow-white giants.

In southern Ontario, the Toronto Zoo closed its polar
bear exhibit in 2007 so that a new and improved one
could be built. There was only one bear left at the zoo
by then, a 27-year-old female named Bisitek. Near the
end of August she was sedated and moved to an

excellent new home — the Polar Bear Habitat in
Cochrane, where Nikita and Aurora, two other bears
from Toronto, were already enjoying their retirement
years. The only work expected of them — and her —
for the rest of their lives is posing for tourists with
cameras.

Cold Comfort

Some world records are far more remarkable than others. But being number one at something ordinary can be fun, as long as it isn't harmful, illegal, or ridiculously dangerous.

Buying, selling and sucking up Slurpees — the frozen, flavoured drinks sold at 7-Eleven stores — is definitely pretty ordinary, but Winnipeggers still think it's fun to be named the Slurpee capital of the world. In 1999, and for the next eight years running, Manitoba's capital earned that title — and a trophy — because a 7-Eleven store in the city sold more Slurpees than any other store in the world. Not only that, in 2007 eight of the top ten Slurpee-selling stores in North America were located in Manitoba.

You might not expect so many people would slurp up so many frozen drinks in a place that's pretty chilly for half the year. But they did. Maybe they suffer from the most brain freezes too.

DID YOU KNOW...

...that icebergs aren't salty? They float in the ocean but they aren't big pieces of frozen sea water. They're huge chunks of ice that break off the edges of glaciers — massive masses of hard-packed snow that build up on land — and drift out to sea.

So, melted iceberg ice isn't salty. And it isn't polluted either, since it comes from glaciers formed thousands of years ago, long before the air was filled with smog. In fact, it's considered to be some of the most drinkable water in the world. That's why icebergs are being "harvested" in Newfoundland. Large sections are broken off, cut into smaller pieces and melted. Then the iceberg water is marketed as exceptionally pure bottled water, and as a key ingredient of some premium beers and vodkas.

Ninety per cent of Newfoundland's icebergs calve, or break away from glaciers, along the west coast of Greenland. Icebergs from there travel an average of about seven kilometres per year, making them some of the fastest-moving icebergs in the world.

A Big Cheese

The first cheese factory in Canada was built in Ingersoll in southwestern Ontario. Within a few years it was producing cheddar as fine as any being made in Europe, and by 1866 factory owner James Harris had decided it was time to let the world know just how tasty Oxford County's cheeses were. So he came up with a plan to promote them in a big way — by making a very big cheese.

Harris had no trouble recruiting two other producers and more than 250 dairy farmers in the area to help him with his plan. Together they collected the coagulated milk solids, or curds, from nearly 32 tonnes of milk from 2400 cows. Then Harris supervised the mixing, pressing and turning of the cheese. After aging for three months, the huge cheese weighing 3310 kilograms was ready to roll.

In August 1866 townsfolk cheered as Harris had it loaded on a train bound for a state fair in Saratoga, New York. It was a huge hit there. People had never seen such a big cheese. Then Harris shipped the massive cheese off on a grand tour of England and Europe. After several weeks travelling from city to city, it was bought by a wholesaler in Liverpool, England, who cut it up and sold it to small shops and individual cheese lovers. But a 40-kilogram chunk was returned to Ingersoll, where one small piece of it is still on display in the Ingersoll Cheese Factory Museum.

Cheesy, and Proud of It

James McIntyre, the owner of a furniture factory in Ingersoll, Ontario, in the second half of the 19th century, loved both cheese and writing poetry. The pairing of those two passions led to his being known as Canada's cheese poet. These days he's also considered by many to be Canada's worst poet, and it's not hard to see why.

In verse after bad verse, McIntyre sang the praises of dairy farming, cows, milk, cream, cheese, cheese and more cheese. When Ingersoll's monster cheese headed off on its grand tour, McIntyre was thrilled. He was also inspired to compose a poem honouring it and the cows that produced the milk to make it. A few verses from that poem, titled *Ode on the Mammoth Cheese*, show why some newspaper editors didn't take McIntyre's work seriously, but published some of his poems anyway to give their readers a laugh.

> We have seen thee, queen of cheese,
> Lying quietly at your ease,
> Gently fanned by evening breeze,
> Thy fair form no flies dare seize.
>
> * * *
>
> Cows numerous as a swarm of bees,
> Or as the leaves upon the trees,
> It did require to make thee please,
> And stand unrivalled, queen of cheese.

We'rt thou suspended from balloon,
You'd cast a shade even at noon,
Folks would think it was the moon
About to fall and crush them soon.

That image of the giant cheese falling from the sky to crush people isn't just bad poetry — it's downright scary. Death by cheese? No poet should go there, not even one of the world's worst.

A Really Big Cheese

Nearly 30 years after the big cheese from Ingersoll, Ontario, made its debut, one from Perth, Ontario, came along that made it look puny. Known as The Mammoth Cheese from Perth, it was nearly 2 metres high and 8.5 metres around, and weighed in at 9980 kilograms — more than three times heavier than the Ingersoll cheese. One year in the making, it was ready just in time to travel by train on a special flatbed car to the Chicago World Expo in 1893.

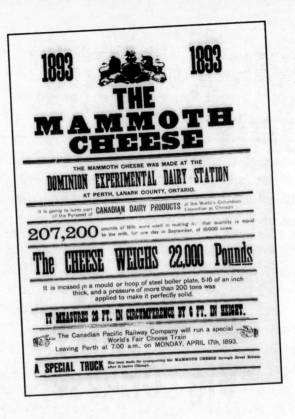

The cheese was the talk of the fair, and rightly so: it was the largest cheese in the world. That record stood until 1964, when a round of cheddar from Wisconsin, USA, tipped the scales at 15 853 kilograms at the New York World's Fair.

Perth is still proud of its giant cheese. A piece is proudly displayed at the museum here, and there's even a full-size concrete replica of it near the railway tracks.

Them's Fightin' Words

Perth, Ontario, holds another place in Canada's history — as the site where the last duel to the death in Canada was fought. It was here that two young law students, Robert Lyon and John Wilson, came face to face early on the morning of June 13, 1833, because of a quarrel over a supposed insult to a young lady in town.

Both men's first shots were misses, so their quarrel should have ended then with a simple apology. But pride and foolishness got the better of them, and they stepped apart and fired their pistols again. This time Wilson's bullet found its mark and Lyon fell to the ground mortally wounded.

At the time no one could have known that that particular duel to the death would be Canada's last. But because it was, the set of pistols Lyon and Wilson used are on display in the Perth Museum.

Critter Crossing

Banff National Park in Alberta is the only national park in North America with a major highway — the Trans-Canada Highway — cutting right through it. Tourists and residents appreciate the highway, but for wildlife in the park, it can be a deadly trap.

During the 1980s the road east of Banff was upgraded to a four-lane divided highway. Eleven underpasses were created to provide safe, car-free ways for animals to cross. In the late 1990s the 35-kilometre section of highway west of Banff was expanded too. Another 11 underpasses were built and 2.4-metre-high fences were erected well back from the road. Two new — and very different — overpasses were also constructed, each costing about $1.5 million. They, and all the underpasses, were put in place at key locations where animals were more likely to try to cross the road.

The new overpasses are not meant to carry vehicles. Intended for four-legged pedestrians, they are, in effect, elevated footpaths as wide as football fields. They slope gently upward as they approach the highway, and they're covered with dirt, grass, bushes, shrubs and short trees. The idea is to make them look like hilly extensions of the woods and meadows that border the road. The mounded earth and the shrubs and trees growing along the edges block distant views of the road and form a natural sound barrier that muffles traffic noise.

During the first year that the million-dollar overpasses were in place, just one black bear and one cougar crossed over them. Later, researchers would discover that black bears and cougars prefer using the narrower, more enclosed underpasses. But after a few years, more and more animals, especially grizzly bears, moose, deer, elk and wolves, started using the wide pathways meant to reduce their chances of ending up as roadkill. Now, if people could only come up with road signs the animals could follow . . .

...that Saskatchewan is the only province with an official sport?

Canada has two official sports — hockey and lacrosse. In 2001 the Saskatchewan government decided to have one too, and voted to give curling that special status because the sport is so popular in the province and to honour the many national, world and Olympic championship performances by star stone throwers from Saskatchewan.

Pricey Panties

On July 30, 2008, Barbara Rusch, a Toronto, Ontario, property manager, bid $9000 by phone on an item being auctioned off thousands of kilometres away in Derby, England, and she was delighted when the auctioneer said, "Sold!"

Rusch had just bought a very expensive pair of underpants that were more than 100 years old. The underpants were large — 110 centimetres wide. They had to be, because their former owner had been a big lady. Rusch was a collector fascinated by the 19th century, and she had just paid $9000 for a pair of Queen Victoria's bloomers.

A Grouch's Home Sweet Home

Every town needs one. That's what the residents of Evansburg, Alberta, decided when they erected a sign welcoming visitors. The sign said Evansburg was home to lots of friendly people — and one grouch. The way folks saw it, admitting there was one cranky resident took the pressure off everybody else to be friendly all the time. Just for the fun it, in 1979 the townspeople voted to select a real live official town grouch, and they've been doing it ever since. The person chosen can be as annoying as he or she dares to be for a whole year. There's also a large wooden Grouch Bench in town where someone feeling grouchy can sit and grumble, but only for one hour. The time limit is clearly displayed on a sign on the bench.

The biggest...

bicycle festival in the world is held every year in Montreal, Quebec, from the end of May through the first few days of June.

Bike lovers from across Canada and around the world join thousands of Montrealers to herald the beginning of summer with Bike Fest, a five-day celebration of cycling. Some people come for the parties and concerts, others for the picnics and family-friendly cycling tours, but almost all of them are there for the Fest's two main events.

About 12 000 riders join in the fun of a *Tour la Nuit* on the Friday night — a 20-kilometre ride, not a race, through downtown streets. With their bike lights on, they look like a river of yellow and red flowing quietly through the darkness. As many as 30 000 people register and line up to take part in the other main event on Sunday, the *Tour de l'Île de Montréal*. It's a 50-kilometre marathon around the island, led out by the serious riders who are followed by the wildest collection of old, new, big and small bikes and riders. The cyclists are there for the fun of it, and so are the cheering crowds that line the route. Ride on!

The largest...

car park in the world is the lot at the West Edmonton Mall in Edmonton, Alberta. It has room for 20 000 cars, vans, SUVs, station wagons and pickup trucks.

Tempting the Tide

A very unusual competitive run is held at Five Islands, Nova Scotia, off the shore of Colchester County on the Bay of Fundy. The "Not Since Moses" Walk and Run takes place the first week of July on the day of the lowest tide of the year. Dick Lemon, a California resident who bought Long Island — one of the Five Islands — in 2003, organized the first event in 2007 as a way of sharing the beauty of his new island paradise, and to raise funds for local organizations. It's also a way to give participants the experience of a lifetime.

There's just one day in the year when the tide is low enough that you can manage to reach Long Island by walking on the ocean floor, and that's the day of the run. But you can't dawdle along the way! Whether you enter the five-kilometre walk or run, or the ten-kilometre run, you have to sign a waiver, or legal form, saying you understand the perils involved in participating. As one section of the form reads:

I am aware that because the tides in the area are extreme (going in one six-hour cycle from virtually no tide to 15 meters of water), getting from the start of the event to its finish must occur within strict nature-set limits.

So far, all brave souls have made it to the finish line without dog-paddling for their lives.

...that each July and August up to 2.5 million shorebirds heading south for their winter migration gather in New Brunswick's Bay of Fundy, the site of the world's highest tides?

They stay at several places along the shore for a few weeks so they can feed and build up strength before setting out on their incredibly long, non-stop flight to South America. Like a busy service centre on a major highway, the bay is a reliable and plentiful source of food for the birds. When the tide is out, the exposed seabed teems with tasty morsels they can snap up and gulp down with very little effort.

The waves of birds landing on the beaches and roosting in the trees at Hopewell Rocks Park later in the summer are an amazing added attraction for tourists coming to see the world-famous tides and Flower Pot Rocks. But visitors are asked not to get so close to the birds that they disturb them and make them waste precious energy they'll need for their big trip.

TIED TIDES

The Bay of Fundy is not the only place in Canada to lay claim to the world's highest tides. In 2002 a measurement taken at the Leaf Basin on the southwest corner of Ungava Bay in northern Quebec recorded a tide one centimetre higher than the 16-metre-high tide in the Guinness Book of World Records at the time. But that measurement was never officially recognized. Since then further measurements reveal that tides in the Minas Basin on the Nova Scotia shore of the Bay of Fundy have reached 17 metres, and that those near the village of Tasiujaq on Leaf Bay can reach 16.8 metres. So, with just a mere 20 centimetres separating these record highs, residents of Tasiujaq feel they're entitled to claim that Ungava Bay is tied with Bay of Fundy when it comes to the world's highest tides. It's definitely a close second!

He's the King of the Castle

Lendrum Place is a quiet residential neighbourhood in southwest Edmonton, Alberta. So the one-storey house with the two-storey castle on top of its attached garage is bound to turn heads when people first see it.

The castle wasn't there when a dentist named Ken Wallace bought the house. But after his two daughters were born, he decided that he'd build them a playroom above the garage. When he started the project in the summer of 1980, he was just thinking that his kids

would have a lot of fun playing in a room that looked like a castle. By the time he was done, he had built a major addition to the house complete with turrets, mounted cannons, stained glass windows and an armoured knight standing guard on the roof. Inside he installed a working fireplace and a spiral staircase leading to a large loft-like balcony from which any young Rapunzel could pretend to let down her hair. And over the years he furnished it with antiques he found that fitted in with his castle theme.

Wallace's daughters loved their playroom and, years later, his grandchildren did too. When Wallace retired and moved to warmer Arizona, USA, one of his daughters moved into the house, and her children were thrilled to be able to play in their grandfather's castle whenever they wanted.

Mars on Earth

Space scientists are always on the lookout for new places on Earth where they can conduct experiments to help humans prepare for trips to Mars. In the 1990s a small group of them working with NASA were pleased to find what they thought would be an ideal place to study how humans will explore the red planet when they get there.

It was a polar desert — cold, windy and dry, just like Mars. Its valleys and canyons were similar to those on Mars. Its rocky landscape had been shaped by ice ages long ago, probably just as Mars's landscape had been. It had a large impact crater caused by a high-speeding meteor or comet smashing into the earth, and Mars has many such craters. Even its dirt was reddish, as is the fine layer of iron oxide — rust — that covers much of Mars.

The list of similarities went on and on, and the researchers agreed that they had found a nearly perfect stand-in for Mars — Devon Island, Nunavut, in the high Arctic north of Baffin Island.

...that the Stanley Cup — the National Hockey League's Championship trophy — has become quite the world traveller? Since every player on the winning team is entitled to have it visit his hometown, the Cup has been to hundreds of cities and towns across Canada, the United States and Europe. The Cup has a faithful travelling companion when it's on the move. The Keeper of the Cup, an employee of the Hockey Hall of Fame in Toronto, takes care of it on all its road trips.

Stanley Who?

In April 2006, in hopes of building up interest in hockey in Britain, someone got the bright idea of sending the trophy to the hometown of Lord Stanley of Preston, the Governor General of Canada who donated the silver cup in 1892. Michael Bolt, the Keeper of the Cup, was happy to accept that assignment, but after a day or two in London, England, he wasn't so sure that the trip was going to be a public relations success.

He did attract some attention as he walked, cabbed, and bused the large, shiny, heavy trophy around London, because TV camera crews were following him around, but the presence of the magnificent silver symbol of Canada's national sport barely raised an eyebrow. Most people had no idea what it was. Many of them didn't know who Lord Stanley was either.

But every now and then, Bolt would hear a shout or a cheer as an amazed tourist from Canada recognized the Cup and wondered what the heck it was doing there.

The handwritten lyrics sheet reads (approximately):

Everybodies talking bout
Bagism
Shagism
Dragism
Madism
Ragism
Tagism
Thisism
That-ism

ministers
sinisters
bannisters
cannisters
Bishop +
Fishop
Rabbiop
Popeyes
Bye Byes

resolution
evolution
revolution
flagellation
regulations
integration
meditations
United Nations
Congratulations

John + Yoko
Timmy Leary
Tommy Smothers
Bobby Dylan
Tommy Cooper
Derek Taylor
Norman Mailer
Alan Ginsberg
Hare Krishna
Hare Krishna

All we are saying is give peace a chance

Making Music in Montreal

Gail Renard, who grew up in Montreal, Quebec, was 16 when the Beatles' lead singer, John Lennon, and his soon-to-be wife, Yoko Ono, arrived in Montreal in May 1969 for a "bed in" in support of world peace. Lennon and Ono stayed in bed for eight days at the Queen Elizabeth Hotel, giving reporters interviews and receiving other entertainers who wanted the United States to end the war with Vietnam.

Montreal was buzzing with news of John Lennon's presence in the city, and crowds of fans gathered in front of the hotel every day in hopes of seeing their idol. Gail Renard was one of those fans. One night she and a girlfriend managed to sneak up some back stairs and a fire escape, and fool a security guard into letting them into Lennon's suite.

Instead of having them thrown out right away, the pyjama-wearing Lennon chatted with them briefly, then grabbed a piece of thin cardboard and wrote the lyrics to a song on it in black marker. Then, just before the girls left, he handed the card to Renard, telling her it was going to be worth something one day.

The words Lennon had written on the card were for a song that he, Yoko Ono and about four dozen guests crowded into the suite were about to record on June 1, 1969.

Thirty-nine years later, Gail Renard decided to sell her favorite Beatles souvenir. On July 10, 2008, at an auction in London, England, someone paid more than $830 000 for Lennon's handwritten words to "Give Peace a Chance."

In 2007 children in Canada sent 1.2
million letters to Santa Claus at the
North Pole. Santa also got 45 000 emails
at his Canada Post website. More than 11 000 current
and retired Canada Post employees volunteer to help
Santa sort all those letters. Santa has a real talent
when it comes to learning to speak many languages. He
can answer his mail in 26 different languages.

A Helping Hand from Canada

In November 1981, Canadarm — a 15-metre-long
remotely controlled robotic arm — was first launched
into space aboard the space shuttle Columbia. Built by
Spar Aerospace Limited of Brampton, Ontario, it was
used to pick up and move large objects out of or into
the space shuttle. Since then it has been used on
shuttles to launch and collect satellites and the giant
Hubble space telescope.

In 2001 Canadarm 2, a new and improved version of the
Canadarm, was delivered to the International Space
Station. While the Canadarm was attached to one end
of a space shuttle, the 17.6-metre-long Canadarm 2 can
move around the space station on tracks, allowing

astronauts or engineers remotely controlling it on Earth to continue building and servicing the station. It can be used to do fairly delicate tasks, but it's also strong enough to move a 105-tonne space shuttle.

And in March 2008, Dextre — another Canadian-made robotic body part — was installed on the space station. Looking somewhat like a headless, legless torso, it can ride the same tracks that Canadarm 2 uses or it can be held by the Canadarm and moved around so that its two very nimble, 3-metre-long arms can do all sorts of jobs in space. The dexterous, or agile, Dextre is also loaded with tools, TV cameras, lights and gripper jaws and, like the Canadarms, can be used by astronauts on the space station or remotely controlled from Earth. Not surprisingly, because it can be attached to Canadarm 2, Dextre is also known as the Canada Hand.

OTTAWA
4150 Km

The most...

northerly military establishment in the world is the Canadian Forces Station (CFS) located at Alert, Nunavut, at the very top of Ellesmere Island in the Canadian Arctic. CFS Alert is also the most northerly settlement where people live permanently.

In keeping with how far north and isolated Alert is, military personnel posted there for just three to six months at a time jokingly call themselves the "frozen chosen." The station also has a fitting Inuktitut motto, *Inuit Nunangata Ungata*, which translates into English

as, "the people of the land beyond the land beyond."
Alert really is beyond the beyond. It's 725 kilometres
north of the nearest Inuit settlement at Grise Fjord,
and 4150 kilometres north of Ottawa.

DID
YOU
KNOW...

...that the first recorded discovery of gold in
Canada was made in Quebec in 1846 — at least
10 years before it was discovered in British
Columbia? In 1846 (some sources say
1834) a young girl named Clothilde
Gilbert was crossing a stream near the
Chaudière River, about 80 kilometres south of
Quebec City, when she noticed something
shiny on the shore — a gold nugget about
the size of a small prune. The discovery
caused quite a stir at first, but since little else was found
beyond that day, Gilbert's lucky find didn't lead to a rush for
gold.

Butt Out or Else

From 1676 to 1759 it was against the law for
Quebecers to smoke on the street. Walking around with
tobacco in your pocket was also illegal. The punishment
for being caught was a whipping with a cat-o'-nine-tails
— nine ropes attached at one end to form a most
unpleasant weapon.

Cross-Border Claim to Fame

The author who became known as "the Father of American Humour" in the 1830s and '40s was actually a Canadian from Nova Scotia named Thomas Chandler Haliburton. Haliburton became a lawyer in 1815, and went on to become a very well-respected politician and judge in Nova Scotia. He was also a writer whose popularity as an author soared when a collection of essays he had written for a magazine was published in Halifax in 1836.

The book, *The Clockmaker; or, The Sayings and Doings of Samuel Slick, of Slickville*, featured a fictional character named Sam Slick, an American clockmaker travelling around Nova Scotia who was always coming up with wise words. *The Clockmaker* was a hit in the United States and England as well as in Canada. Sam's words of wisdom became so popular that Haliburton, a Canadian, became America's most frequently quoted author.

In fact, Sam's sayings have been repeated so often that they've become part of the English language. People don't realize that they're quoting the famous fictional Yankee traveller when they say...

It's like looking for a needle in a haystack.

You can't get blood out of a stone.

Never look a gift horse in the mouth.

It's raining cats and dogs.

I wasn't born yesterday.

Seeing is believing.

Quick as a wink!

The longest...

hockey game in the world was played outdoors just east of Edmonton, Alberta, in February 2008.

Brent Sakik, the optometrist who organized the event to raise funds for cancer research, flooded a regulation-size rink in his backyard and lined up needed supplies and volunteers. Then, on February 8, he joined 39 other players ready to brave nose-numbing temperatures for at least a few minutes longer than 240 hours — the world record they were aiming to break.

The two teams of 20 players each kept the game going day and night, with weather ranging from a wind-chilled − 40ºC to an ice-melting 0ºC, and despite numbed fingers and toes, cramping leg muscles, and blistered heels. Finally, on February 18, with TV cameras rolling and scores of friends and strangers cheering them on, 40 exhausted men played the marathon's final hour — hour number 241 — an hour longer than the existing longest game. They had broken the world record, and had raised more than $300 000 while they did it.

Soft as Silk and Smooth as Satin

On September 8, 2008, a line of elegant models strolled down a runway in Toronto wearing stunning creations from eight of Canada's finest fashion designers. *The White Cashmere Collection 2008* was the fifth annual fashion show sponsored by Kruger Products of Canada, and the second such show to feature a special Kruger product. In both 2007 and 2008 all the designers participating in the show had to use sheets of the same "fabric" — Cashmere, Kruger's top-selling toilet tissue.

Hot Potato

In July 2008 Agriculture Canada released the Exploits, a new variety of potato bred in Canada by Kenneth G. Proudfoot, a retired plant-breeding researcher from St. John's, Newfoundland. The creamy-white, tasty Exploits was developed to resist potato wart and virus infections and attacks from golden nematodes, diseases that plague potato-growing efforts in Newfoundland. The breed is fittingly named after the Exploits, the longest river on the island of Newfoundland.

Hard Potato

Maugerville, New Brunswick, has a potato that can resist every wart, virus and bug that tries to attack it. It doesn't sprout eyes or get soft and black in the winter, and it never has to be peeled. It just has to stand tall, wearing a big smile and sporting a top hat, waving at people passing by Harvey's roadside market. Known as Harvey's Big Potato Man, the cheery fellow is made of cement and is six metres tall.

One Banana,
Two Banana,
Three Banana,
Four...

In any other store window, it would have looked like any other banana. But the banana that people walked past in the summer of 2008 was in the window of the Gallery Page and Strange on Granville Street in Halifax, Nova Scotia, and it had a $2500 price tag beside it. So this wasn't just any banana. This banana was art.

Titled "Banana Installation," the display was the creation of Michael Fernandes, an instructor at the Nova Scotia College of Art and Design. He first put a ripe yellow banana on the windowsill on June 13. Then, every day or two, he replaced it with a slightly greener one, until on the last day, July 4, a very green banana lay on the sill. Fernandes ate the bananas he removed, often sharing them with gallery co-owners Victoria Page and Victoria Strange. Only the last banana would go to the buyer, together with daily photos of the window display.

But things didn't go quite as planned. On June 16, when Fernandes showed up at the gallery to replace the banana, he found an apple in its place. Over the weekend, pranksters had stolen the banana, leaving behind a note saying it was a terrorist threat. Fernandes was not amused. And he wasn't too pleased when his creation didn't sell either — although he did get two nibbles. Until gallery owners changed his mind, he had planned to ask $15 000 for it.

DID YOU KNOW...

...that, at one point in the 1980s, fan interest in the Ottawa Rough Riders Canadian Football League (CFL) team was so low that the players bought 7000 tickets to a home game with their own money?

They figured that giving away the tickets would boost interest and bring the team some good publicity. Maybe it did in the long run. But only 1500 or so fans took them up on their offer of free tickets to that game.

Even the Saskatchewan Roughriders, often called the most-loved team in the CFL, were struggling financially in the 1980s. Before the 1987 season opened, the team's management offered season's tickets to farmers in exchange for a tonne of wheat.

A Test of Fan Loyalty

No matter how long it's been since the Toronto Maple Leafs hockey team won the Stanley Cup, the team's fans stick with them through thick and thin. But on March 19, 1981, 14 years after the Leafs had won their last championship, their loyalty was sadly tested as they suffered through the first period of a game against the Buffalo Sabres. In that period the Sabres scored nine goals, the most ever scored in just one period. But that wasn't the only blow to the Leafs' morale that night. They scored four goals, but by the time the game ended, the Sabres had chalked up *fourteen*, the most goals ever scored against the Leafs in a single game.

Better Late than Never

For as long as he could remember, Lyall Gow, a World War II veteran from Ottawa, Ontario, had wanted to parachute from a plane. So when a friend who was a pilot offered to take him up for a jump, Gow leaped at the chance. He arranged to make the jump strapped to a tandem diving instructor from the Gananoque Sport Parachuting Centre in Gananoque, Ontario, just east of Kingston.

On Saturday, June 28, 2008, Gow showed up at the Centre accompanied by about two dozen family and friends, waving to them as he boarded the plane. Soon the plane was airborne and, not long after, Gow jumped, along with the trainer, experiencing the thrill of free-falling for two minutes before the parachute opened.

After Gow had landed safely, he joked about how he might jump again in five years — when he turned 100. When he made the jump he was nearly 96 years old!

The youngest...

radio show host in the world is Dakota "Cody" Morton of Port Alberni, British Columbia.

Morton was born in Calgary, Alberta, on June 12, 1988. Ten years and 218 days later, on January 16, 1999, he made it into the Guinness World Records book as the world's youngest host of a radio program.

Morton's show was called Bust a Groove, and he hosted it live every Saturday morning at CHOO FM in Tofino, British Columbia, where he and his family were living at the time. When they moved to Port Alberni, B.C., Morton got a regular slot for his show at a local radio station. He also reported on special events for other radio stations, and made guest appearances on CTV and MTV shows. When he covered the Juno Awards ceremonies in Hamilton, Ontario, in 2001, he was the youngest person ever to receive official access to the media room.

Made to Honour

The first time Canada sent troops into combat overseas was in the fall of 1899. The British government had asked for help fighting the Boers — people of Dutch descent — in South Africa.

More than 7000 Canadians served during the Boer War (1899-1902). The first 1000 arrived in December 1899, in time to be involved in a major battle two months later at Paardeberg, about 1000 kilometres north of Capetown. Among the many brave men who fought heroically at Paardeberg, one enlisted private — the lowest military rank — stood out for his efforts. On both February 18 and 28, 1900, Private Richard Rowland Thompson risked his own life going to help some wounded comrades. Weeks after the battle, Thompson became so sick that he was sent home to recover.

A woolly scarf followed him to Canada. The gift had arrived for him in South Africa shortly after he had left. During times of war, knitting warm socks, hats, gloves and scarves was one way mothers, wives and daughters of soldiers, sailors and pilots could take care of their loved ones. Thompson's fringed, dull yellow scarf had been crocheted by an 81-year-old woman in England who wanted to show her personal appreciation for the efforts of men like him. The woman was Queen Victoria.

Crocheting eight such scarves just months before she died was the queen of England's way of honouring troops embattled in South Africa. She made four scarves for British soldiers, and one each for "the most distinguished private soldier" from Australia, New Zealand, South Africa and Canada — the four Commonwealth countries that had answered Britain's call for help. Officers who had observed or learned of Thompson's actions at Paardeberg had selected him as Canada's most distinguished private, and the scarf was properly presented to him when it followed him home.

In 1965 the scarf was presented to Canada at a special parliamentary ceremony. It has been proudly displayed at the Canadian War Museum ever since.

A for Effort

On September 15, 2007, more than 500 Boy Scouts from southern Alberta and southeastern British Columbia gathered at the zoo in Calgary, Alberta, in search of a new world record. At the zoo they were joined by a group of students from SAIT (Southern Alberta Institute of Technology) who had brought along two machines they had designed and made specifically for the Scouts.

The record the Scouts wanted to break was for the most popcorn popped in eight hours, and the machines that the engineering and technology students had made were two giant popcorn makers.

The Scouts filled the poppers with kernels and at exactly 8:02 a.m., turned them on. All day long they carted away big buckets of popcorn that the poppers kept popping at a rate of 57 litres a minute. At exactly 4:02 p.m., everybody involved stopped. The number of buckets was totalled and that number was multiplied by the volume of popcorn each one held. The final calculation showed that the Scouts had popped an amazing 34 000 litres — or 34 cubic metres — of exploded kernels.

Unfortunately for the Scouts, the existing record was 48 420 litres — or 48.42 cubic metres. They weren't even close.

Fortunately for the elephants, gorillas and other zoo residents, the popcorn was all theirs to eat.

They Made It!

On July 24, 1988, a much smaller group of Albertans — about two dozen — set out to break another world record. Led by Mike Rogiani, the so-called "ice cream king" of Edmonton, the group filled an empty swimming pool temporarily installed in the West Edmonton Mall with truckloads of 65 different flavours of ice cream and 6 different flavours — butterscotch, strawberry, chocolate, pineapple, caramel and fudge — of sticky, yummy sauces. Then they topped it all off with dozens of litres of whipped cream covered in peanut sprinkles and juicy red cherries.

The ginormous pool of ice cream weighed in at 24.91 tonnes (about 25 000 kilograms), a new world record for an ice cream sundae.

Thousands of spectators showed up that Sunday to see Rogiani's edible masterpiece, and many of them paid $1 for a two-litre pailful. Rogiani and his team of family and friends sold about 5000 pails, with all the sales going to support a children's ward in a local hospital.

It took about four hours to make the sundae. It took about eight hours to clean up afterward.

Walking the Line

Stanstead, Quebec, is a small town about 150 kilometres east of Montreal on the border with the state of Vermont, USA. Derby Line, Vermont, is a small town about 150 kilometres east of Montreal on the border with the province of Quebec, Canada.

But the two towns aren't just close together — they are actually *joined* together in places. They even share certain streets and buildings. In fact, the Haskell Free Library and Opera House, the main building in both towns, was deliberately constructed on the border between them in 1901 to show how well the people could get along.

But the border between Stanstead and Derby Line isn't just the property line between the two towns. The border between them is THE border — the international boundary between Canada and the United States.

For years residents going about their regular business didn't worry too much about which side of the line they were on. They weren't concerned about crossing the border to visit a next-door neighbour, to move around the shared library, or to go in the front door of an apartment building and out the back way. They didn't even think about the fact that the kitchens in some houses were in one country and the dining rooms were in

the other. And Americans living on the south side of Canusa Street, which is in Canada, didn't check in with a border guard every time they backed out of their driveways and entered Canada.

But after the terrorist attacks in the United States on September 11, 2001, the American government began doing a lot more to strengthen control of the country's border crossings. Security cameras were installed to monitor the three unguarded streets that cross the border, and sensors were placed in the streets to detect cars driving across. People who did cross had to report what they'd done to American or Canadian border officials at one of three guarded crossings as soon as possible, or they would be tracked down and questioned.

Townsfolk also had to start reporting that they were about to enter or leave Canada or the United States before they crossed certain streets to do their shopping. And since the entrances to the library and theatre are in the United States, if people ever had to run out a back exit in case of an emergency, they'd have to report *that* border crossing to officials right away too.

DID YOU KNOW...

...that the action-filled movie *Shanghai Noon* (2000), starring Jackie Chan, Owen Wilson and Lucy Liu wasn't filmed in the "wild west" of the American state of Nevada, as the plot indicates? It was filmed in Alberta, mainly in Calgary and the badlands around Drumheller.

The musical hit *Hairspray* (2007), starring John Travolta, Queen Latifah and Michelle Pfeiffer, appears to take place in Baltimore, Maryland. But Toronto and Hamilton, Ontario, stand in for that American city.

Thousands of Bottles of Beer on the Wall

By the early 2000s fewer than two dozen people —
mainly artists — were living in Keno City, Yukon, east of
Dawson City. A few buildings remain, relics of the years
when it was a small, but thriving, mining town. The
museum is a must-see for anyone who travels to the end
of the Silver Trail highway from Dawson. So is the glass
house where Geordie Dobson once lived.

Years after Dobson opened the Keno City Hotel in 1963,
he ended up with a huge pile of stubby beer bottles

piled up behind the place. Eventually he decided that the time had come to do some serious reusing, and he began building beer bottle walls around the outside of his house. It took Dobson three summers to mortar 32 000 bottles together, but when he was done, he was pleased with the result. Apparently the walls of glass with air trapped inside acted as great insulation.

The largest . . .

slab of fudge in the world was made on May 24, 2007, by Chantelle Gorham at the Northwest Fudge Factory in Sudbury, Ontario.

The melt-in-your-mouth blend of cream, butter, sugar, corn syrup and vegetable oil (plus chocolate in part of it) was nearly 14 metres long, 2 metres wide and 10 centimetres thick, and it weighed 2290 kilograms.

The biggest . . .

lollipop in the world was made on June 25, 2002, at the Hershey Foods factory in Smith Falls, Ontario.

The candy on a stick was a huge cherry-flavoured Jolly Rancher Fruit Chew that was 160 centimetres square, 48 centimetres thick and weighed in at 1821.63 kilograms.

A Cookie Monster's Dream Come True

The bag of cookies that went on display at the Loblaws Wonderland Market in London, Ontario, on September 6, 2001, was definitely a shopper stopper. The huge bag made by Loblaws Supermarkets Ltd. stood 3.29 metres high, was 114.3 centimetres wide and 2.13 metres deep. Loaded up with a grand total of 100 152 chewy chocolate chip cookies, it was the biggest bag of cookies in the world.

A Hard Sell

A lot of snow fell around Montreal before Christmas in 2007, so much so that by the middle of December a massive mound two metres high had built up on Michel Levesque's lawn in the suburb of Sainte-Eustache, Quebec. So, just for the heck of it, on December 18 Levesque put up his "magnificent snowbank" for auction online on eBay, pointing out that his snow would be perfect for ski hills and warning bidders that there would be no refunds or returns. And he let it be known that he would be sending all the proceeds to a charity called Operation Enfants Soleil that helps children in hospitals.

As Levesque expected, the opening bid was for 99 cents, but the price quickly went up from there, especially after his weird posting on eBay made the news. When the bidding ended, it had reached $3550!

Levesque was disappointed when he found out that the top bid was a hoax. But the next day Sophie Rouillier and Claude Fraser, a couple who had bid the second-highest amount, ended up buying the snowbank for $3000 — and even topping that up with another $550 to match the original false bid.

Levesque was very pleased with how well his wacky idea had paid off, at least from a fundraising point of view. Unfortunately the new owners never arrived to collect their purchase, so he was still stuck with all that snow.

Just the Stats

On average, one half hour spent shovelling snow burns about 410 calories. Raking leaves or washing the car for the same length of time burns about 150 calories and sleeping for 30 minutes will only burn 30 calories. But that means sleeping for eight hours would burn off 480 calories. Hmm... shovelling snow versus sleeping? Nap time!

A Very Long-Distance Call

After working for months on a radio communications project, Patrick Neelin, Paul Je, Kevin Luong and Gino Cunti were ready to demonstrate it. But they weren't sure it would work. At exactly 12:29 p.m. on February 2, 2009, the four students at Humber College in Toronto, Ontario, "handed it in" and held their breath. At that moment, if all went well, the International Space Station would be in position for ten minutes to receive a scheduled message from the radio system they had designed and built themselves.

At first all they heard was static, so they tried to send a second message. And this time, after a few nerve-wracking seconds, American astronaut Sandra Magnus responded from the orbiting station. For the next few minutes, the four young men were able to ask her some technical questions. Magnus, with degrees in electrical engineering and physics, was happy to answer them. She was also happy for the students. As an astronaut who was also a licensed amateur ham radio operator, she understood completely what they had done and why they had wanted to go for it.

Just the Stats

More than 22 000 schools from 164 different countries took part in the two-day-long online competition held for World Math Day on March 4-5, 2008. One million students entered. Sixty-five of them were from St. Margaret's Public School in Scarborough, Ontario.

When the math competition ended, six Canadian students were in the top 100. And of those top six Canadians, three came from St. Margaret's. Shourav Saha, who was first in Canada, came 20th in the world. Derek Hawkins was second in Canada and 24th in the world, and Sanan Mujadidi placed sixth in Canada and 76th in the world.

Shourav Saha, first in Canada, was in Grade 5 at St. Margaret's when he entered the competition. During the two days online, he had 44 000 right answers, answering correctly about 75 questions a minute!

Photo Credits